LEVEL FOUR · Chapters

Learning to read. Reading to learn!

LEVEL ONE Sounding It Out Preschool–Kindergarten
For kids who know their alphabet and are starting to sound out words.

learning sight words • beginning reading • sounding out words

LEVEL TWO Reading with Help Preschool–Grade 1
For kids who know sight words and are learning to sound out new words.

expanding vocabulary • building confidence • sounding out bigger words

LEVEL THREE Independent Reading Grades 1–3
For kids who are beginning to read on their own.

introducing paragraphs • challenging vocabulary • reading for comprehension

LEVEL FOUR Chapters Grades 2–4
For confident readers who enjoy a mixture of images and story.

reading for learning • more complex content • feeding curiosity

Ripley Readers Designed to help kids build their reading skills and confidence at any level, this program offers a variety of fun, entertaining, and unbelievable topics to interest even the most reluctant readers. With stories and information that will spark their curiosity, each book will motivate them to start and keep reading.

PUBLISHING

Vice President, Licensing & Publishing Amanda Joiner
Editorial Manager Carrie Bolin

Editor Jordie R. Orlando
Writer Korynn Wible-Freels
Designer Scott Swanson
Reprographics Bob Prohaska
Production Design Luis Fuentes
Proofreader Rachel Paul

Published by Ripley Publishing 2020

10 9 8 7 6 5 4 3 2 1

Copyright © 2020 Ripley Publishing

ISBN: 978-1-60991-458-5

For more information regarding permission, contact:
VP Licensing & Publishing
Ripley Entertainment Inc.
7576 Kingspointe Parkway, Suite 188
Orlando, Florida 32819

Email: publishing@ripleys.com
www.ripleys.com/books
Manufactured in China in May 2020.

First Printing

Library of Congress Control Number:
2020937147

PUBLISHER'S NOTE
While every effort has been made to verify the accuracy of the entries in this book, the Publisher cannot be held responsible for any errors contained in the work. They would be glad to receive any information from readers.

Ripley Readers

Take Flight!

All true and unbelievable!

RIPLEY
PUBLISHING
a Jim Pattison Company

TABLE OF CONTENTS

CHAPTER 1
DREAMS OF FLIGHT

High among the clouds you see a tiny, distant **airplane**. It is carrying people across the world in just a matter of hours! Have you ever wondered when giant jetliners started soaring through the sky? Let's take a look at the human history of flight!

People have wanted a bird's-eye view for thousands of years! One old Greek myth tells the story of a man named Icarus flying with wings made of feathers and wax.

In 1893, German inventor Otto Lilienthal flew one of his handmade **gliders** for over 1,000 feet!

Believe It or Not! Special man-lifting kites were once used for military spying and for entertainment!

10

The **Renaissance** was a famous time for art, education, and... airplanes? Leonardo da Vinci began sketching designs for a flying machine back in 1488! These drawings may not look like the aircraft we have today, but da Vinci was closer than any other man of his time to taking flight!

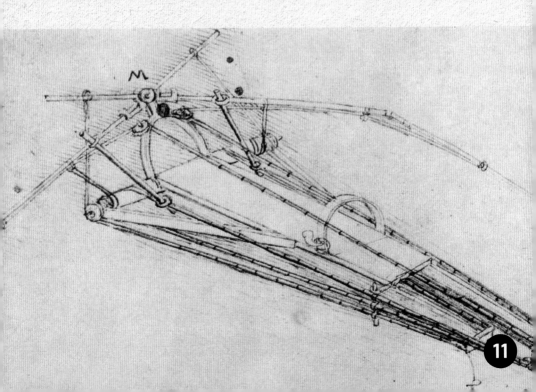

CHAPTER 2
BALLOONS: NOT JUST FOR PARTIES!

Hot air and gas balloons were the earliest modes of air travel! The first manned and **untethered** hot air balloon was launched on November 21, 1783, in Paris. Would you have felt safe using fire to keep your paper balloon in the air?

It took the first gas balloon two and a half hours to travel 25 miles. A jet plane can fly about 1,500 miles in that amount of time!

The famous Goodyear **blimp** is known for flying over football games. But did you know that its cousin the **airship** was designed to carry passengers? Both airships and blimps use gasses to float, but an airship has a sturdy structure to keep its shape.

The Hindenburg was a famous German airship. In 1937, its gasses caught fire and the Hindenburg was destroyed. Airship travel became less popular after the tragedy.

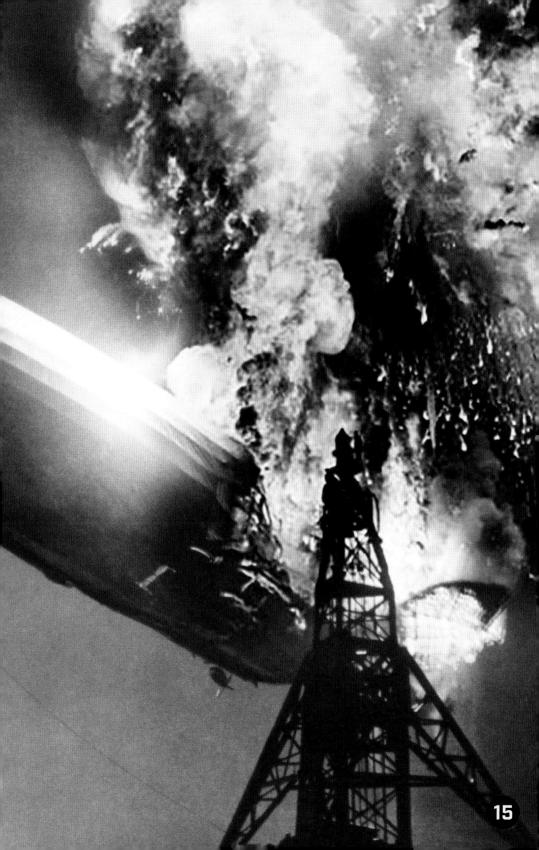

CHAPTER 3
THE WRIGHT STUFF

Take a look at the Flyer 1 and you may not recognize it as an airplane at all! The Flyer 1 was the very first ancestor of today's modern jet planes. It had double-decker wings, and the pilot flew while laying down!

Brothers Wilbur and Orville Wright are known for designing, building, and flying the Flyer 1. Airships were filled with lightweight gasses to make them lighter than the air around them. However, the Flyer 1 plane weighed more than the air! This historic legend traveled for 852 feet in less than a minute, making it the first machine of its kind to fly!

Believe It or Not! The Wright brothers' amazing flight was only reported by four newspapers the next day!

So how do airplanes fly, anyway? As the plane picks up speed on the **runway**, the fast-moving air is forced beneath the wings, pushing the plane up from the ground!

Take a look at the parts of a typical jet plane:

1. **ENGINE**: powers the plane

2. **WINGS**: pushes air toward the ground and holds the plane in the air

3. **WINGLETS**: reduces drag, the force slowing down the plane

4. TAIL: keeps the plane balanced

5. COCKPIT: where the pilot and copilot operate the plane

Turbulence refers to unsteady air. It can be a little scary when a plane starts to shake, but turbulence is normal! Changing wind speeds and hot air from clouds can cause a plane to rattle. Just stay buckled up when the pilot turns on the seat-belt light!

CHAPTER 4
FROM DELIVERIES TO DAREDEVILS

Airplanes were first used for practical reasons, like delivering mail. Take a look at this U.S. airmail carrier. There was no roof to protect the pilot from wind or rain!

In 1913, Katherine Stinson made history as the first female U.S. airmail pilot!

Stamps turned to stunts in the 1920s. Barnstormers were daring people who performed **aerial** tricks to entertain a paying audience! Many World War I pilots found joy in showing off their skills in this way!

Barnstormers got their name by performing their shows at local farms. Some would even fly right through an open barn! Playing tennis on the wings and leaping from plane to plane are just two examples of barnstorming stunts!

Believe It or Not! Mildred Unger danced on the wings of a plane 2,000 feet in the air. Did we mention she was ten years old?

On October 14, 1947, Captain Charles Yeager made history by traveling faster than the speed of sound! This created a **sonic boom** over the Mojave Desert! You can see his airplane, the Glamorous Glennis, at the National Air and Space Museum.

GLAMOROUS GLENNIS

CHAPTER 5
TYPES OF PLANES

TYPE: **Propeller** plane

PURPOSE: transporting passengers or cargo for short distances

FIRST USED: 1903

FUN FACT: Crop dusters are propeller planes that spread fertilizer over farming fields.

TYPE: Commercial jet airliner

PURPOSE: transports passengers or cargo for long distances

FIRST USED: 1952

FUN FACT: Peanuts, pretzels, and Biscoff cookies are the three most common airline snacks. Yum!

TYPE: Military fighter jet

PURPOSE: used in aerial warfare

FIRST USED: 1914, during World War I

FUN FACT: The F-15 can reach speeds of almost 2,000 miles per hour!

TYPE: Seaplanes

PURPOSE: designed to land on water

FIRST USED: 1910

FUN FACT: The first round-the-world seaplane trip was unplanned and happened from December 1941 through January 1942, following the attack on Pearl Harbor.

TYPE: Stealth planes

PURPOSE: to fly undetected for military purposes

FIRST USED: 1989

FUN FACT: The B-2 stealth bomber can be refueled in the air. On one mission, two B-2s stayed airborne for 32 hours.

TYPE: NASA's reduced-gravity aircraft (called the Vomit Comet)

PURPOSE: to train astronauts, to conduct research, and for entertainment

FIRST USED: 1957

FUN FACT: You can experience the Vomit Comet yourself for the "low" price of $5,000 a ride!

CHAPTER 6
OTHER WAYS TO FLY

Though airplanes may be the most popular type of air travel, there are several other ways to soar high in the sky!

A helicopter has a large spinning blade on its top and a small spinning blade on its tail. These are called *rotors*. Helicopters are great for landing in small spaces because they don't need runways!

Helicopters can transport hospital patients, spread water over forest fires, rescue flood victims from rooftops, and pick up hikers on a narrow mountain path.

Flying is out of this world... literally! The first space rocket took people to the moon in 1969. A rocket produces over one million pounds of thrust, which is the force that moves an aircraft.

The Soyuz Rocket is a Russian spacecraft that takes people to the International Space Station. The ISS has at least three astronauts aboard at all times!

Believe It or Not!
Only 66 years after the very first airplane, the Saturn V rocket helped take astronauts all the way to the moon!

Want the excitement of flying without the passengers and peanuts? **Wingsuits** allow you soar through the air with your own set of wings! This kind of flying requires a lot of special training. Wingsuit flyers can reach up to 100 miles per hour!

CHAPTER 7

THE FUTURE OF FLIGHT

Did you know that a jumbo jet engine uses one gallon of fuel every second? In hopes of cutting back on fuel use and **pollution**, Switzerland is experimenting with airplanes designed to run only on solar power! Solar power uses energy from the sun to power technology. In 2016, the aircraft called the Solar Impulse 2 traveled around the world with the sun as its only power source!

Don't panic—this is no alien invasion! A Romanian inventor has produced an all-directional flying object! This amazing invention does exactly what the name says: it flies in all directions! Who knows? In 50 years, an airport could look like an alien fleet!

Human flight has come a long way since hot air balloons first took to the sky! Just like our ancestors who paved the way for planes, our fascination with flying will keep us soaring higher!

aerial: something that happens in the air.

airplane: a powered flying machine that is heavier than air.

airship: a powered flying machine that is lighter than air.

blimp: a type of airship that uses gas to hold its shape, like a balloon.

glider: a device that flies with no engine.

pollution: anything that does not belong in and harms the environment, like trash or chemicals.

propeller: spinning blades that help lift an aircraft.

Renaissance: a period of history in Europe between the years 1300 and 1600.

runway: the strip of ground that an airplane uses to take off and land.

sonic boom: the loud sound created when something goes faster than the speed of sound.

untethered: not connected to anything.

wingsuit: a special suit with fabric between the arms and legs that allows the wearer to glide through the air.

Ripley Readers

Ready for More?

Ripley Readers feature unbelievable but true facts and stories!

For more information about Ripley's Believe It or Not!, go to www.ripleys.com